1001 Embezzlers

A Study of Defalcations
in Business

UNITED STATES FIDELITY AND GUARANTY COMPANY
BALTIMORE

Copyrighted 1937
United States Fidelity and Guaranty Company
Printed in U. S. A.

Foreword

While it is estimated that employers in the United States lose $200,000,000 yearly through employe dishonesty, yet by choice and by inclination the majority of employes are honest.

Dishonesty, being as old as humanity, is no more a phenomenon of the present times than are the other violations of the Ten Commandments, nor is the embezzler peculiar to any one city, climate, or business. He is usually not of the criminal type. In general, he has held a position of some trust and responsibility and has enjoyed a good reputation.

The findings presented in these pages are drawn from 1,001 case histories of embezzlers—employed men and women who, after previously passing the scrutiny of employer and underwriter, were bonded against dishonesty by this Company. It developed that the judgment passed upon them by employer and underwriter had been wrong—proof that it is impossible to predict with certainty the future actions of any man.

Since our underwriters review in the course of a year the past of some five hundred thousand employes, and for forty years our adjusters have received daily upwards of one hundred dishonesty claims, we may presume to speak, if not with authority, at least with experience.

Aside from the fact that this study should help the underwriter of fidelity bonds, it may be of value as a commentary on human vagaries.

E. ASBURY DAVIS, *President*
United States Fidelity and Guaranty Company

Baltimore, Maryland
December 22, 1936

Portrait

YOUR TYPICAL EMBEZZLER belongs in the white collar class. He is thirty-six years old. He is married. He has a wife and two children. He is not psychopathic or of feeble mind, nor does he live in a neighborhood where crime is widespread. His upbringing has been good. He is not the lowest paid person in his employer's organization, nor is he the highest. His friends and very often his wife imagine that his salary is $300.00 a month or more, but it is nearer $175.00 a month. He has a high school education. He lives comfortably. He has a medium priced automobile, last year's model, on which a balance is still owing. His traveling has been confined to occasional week-ends and a two-week vacation in the summer. He is a good mixer. He participates in social and community affairs. He enjoys a good time. He likes a drink, but he rarely takes it during business hours.

He lives in every state in the Union, in every province of Canada, in large cities, in small cities. He is employed in every type of business. He is competent and smart. He has held his position for five and a half years. His employer regards him favorably and he has *honestly* earned the position of trust to which he has attained. In short, so far as his past record is concerned, he is a regular fellow, a normal individual with a better than average business reputation and future.

..... Yet he becomes an embezzler.

It may be simply that he is a poor business man, or that he obtains or extends credit unwisely. He does not always benefit in the process of the embezzlement.

It may be that he is over ambitious, operating a private business of his own on the side, the demands of which lead him to "borrow" from his employer's funds.

It may be that he has come to feel that he is being unfairly treated and that he is rightly entitled to the money or property which he is taking from his employer. Or, the employer may be lax in supervision and therefore the temptation greater than should be the case.

It may be that in one way or another he permits debts to accumulate and then seeks to ease the pressure of creditors by paying them with his employer's funds.

Your typical embezzler is often overtaken by domestic troubles which lead him to spend beyond his means. He may have a spendthrift or nagging wife or a wife who is an invalid. He may have ailing children or an ambitious family whose demands cannot be met by his income. His family may feel that it has to "keep up with the Jones'." His sons or daughters may have become pressing social or financial problems. His wife may be unfaithful or he himself may fall victim to a consuming infatuation for another woman, which will cause him to spend recklessly.

On the other hand, he may succumb to an overindulgence in liquor—to gambling or speculation, "dipping into the till" or "kiting" his accounts to satisfy his thirst or recoup his losses. In ninety-nine times out of one hundred he is "temporarily borrowing" and would indignantly deny that he is a thief.

Frequently, an unexpected emergency, created by death, sickness, or personal financial loss—he claims as the cause for committing his first but fatal defalcation. He meant to borrow only until the next pay day. After which he may continue for a long period, hoping that some fortuitous circumstance will extricate him from his trouble. When, finally he finds himself hopelessly involved, your typical embezzler is much more likely to commit suicide or break down and confess than he is to abscond. If he does abscond, however, it is usually "with the other woman."

When brought to book he has little or none of the property or money which he embezzled.

Seven

The 1,001 cases of embezzlement are from recent files of the United States Fidelity and Guaranty Company. No attempt was made to hand-pick them. They represent an average cross-section, and therefore, assure a fairly representative picture of embezzlers and embezzling. Results of the study were checked against the accumulated experience of the Company, especially where there was doubt in any particular.

Naturally, no attempt has been made in this study to draw conclusions as to the relative probabilities of a man or woman employe's becoming dishonest. What we deal with herein are actual facts from actual cases. Moreover, there are many instances of restitution which never come to light—where the employe makes good the loss and continues in his employment. Then again there are the countless instances where an employer rather that publicize his loss accepts it as best he may, without recourse to court.

* * *

The tabulations reveal an almost complete geographical distribution. Forty-seven states of the Union, the District of Columbia, most provinces of Canada, as well as several foreign countries where American concerns have branches, are represented.

The types of business constitute a picture of mercantile and industrial life. They include manufacturers of machines, textiles, furniture, specialties and clothes, producers of gasoline, oils, and food products, mining and lumber companies, automobile and moving picture concerns, distributors, brokers and sales agencies; wholesalers and retailers of almost every description. Publishers, theatrical producers, decorators, advertising agencies, newspapers and hotels are also among the employers. In addition, there are building and loan and benefit associations, hospitals, churches, religious and fraternal organizations.

Again, the list includes employes of every degree of importance—from warehouse watchman to president. Many handled the cash of their employers, while a surprisingly large number handled no money, being in positions where possibility of embezzlement would seem remote. Some of the embezzlers were among thousands of employes in their organizations. Others represented the entire office force.

As this study was confined to mercantile embezzlers, no cases of public officials, or government, bank or railroad employes have been included.

Borrowings

Comparatively few embezzlements get into public print and some of the facts disclosed by the accompanying tables may not conform to popular conceptions. Nevertheless, the 963 men and the 38 women who comprise the 1,001 studies were embezzlers, for they got away with more than six million dollars in money and property.

Property as considered here is not limited to money, but is anything of value subject to ownership or possession. An embezzler, therefore, does not necessarily steal actual cash.

The 963 men stole $6,127,588.48 and the 38 women stole $156,918.01. The average man took $6,363.02, the average woman $4,129.42.

Although the employer had bonded his employe as protection against possible embezzlement, the losses sustained were nearly 90 per cent. greater than the amount of protection which had been considered sufficient. In total, the losses exceeded the amount of the bonds by $2,922,316.28. This figure represents the loss to employers and is a measure of their error in judgment regarding the hazard of embezzlement.

Ten

LOCATION OF THE LOSSES
A geographical breakdown of the cases

	NUMBER	DEFALCATIONS	UNDER INSURANCE
Alabama	12	$ 29,972.76	$ 4,781.37
Arizona	4	7,140.66	159.00
Arkansas	12	36,596.85	13,633.82
California	40	289,417.39	140,420.08
Colorado	12	51,409.43	20,099.70
Connecticut	5	12,829.95	3,980.13
Delaware	1	1,130.58	
District of Columbia	8	27,124.47	10,747.69
Florida	29	102,982.43	36,361.15
Georgia	27	1,066,366.14	964,143.82
Idaho	4	18,366.14	3,207.06
Illinois	75	431,793.40	121,283.42
Indiana	16	109,398.48	43,066.78
Iowa	12	26,656.81	2,776.57
Kansas	18	48,465.57	4,104.76
Kentucky	8	44,926.44	18,355.47
Louisiana	17	67,618.13	20,508.19
Maine	1	3,875.63	
Maryland	14	66,638.89	803.39
Massachusetts	18	238,083.53	166,109.82
Michigan	25	108,206.53	51,282.17
Minnesota	17	52,133.52	17,171.78
Mississippi	17	56,231.46	12,185.73
Missouri	20	111,375.75	40,321.59
Montana	7	12,848.04	1,417.40
Nebraska	4	8,978.23	1,196.33
Nevada	2	25,056.57	3,742.75
New Hampshire	2	3,268.04	627.35

Continued

Continued

LOCATION OF THE LOSSES

	NUMBER	DEFALCATIONS	UNDER INSURANCE
New Jersey	27	$ 121,996.22	$ 33,701.47
New Mexico	5	11,504.02	
New York	141	1,049,189.23	327,098.76
North Carolina	12	40,661.60	12,846.70
North Dakota	5	8,034.47	
Ohio	35	170,880.13	59,661.50
Oklahoma	31	130,265.88	65,245.00
Oregon	7	38,890.27	6,367.89
Pennsylvania	40	170,193.45	74,734.17
South Carolina	11	28,013.16	7,965.29
South Dakota	4	18,259.61	
Tennessee	7	110,277.40	5,709.96
Texas	60	240,389.30	87,602.09
Utah	6	13,694.72	2,958.56
Vermont	2	5,920.26	3,200.00
Virginia	10	20,388.80	2,031.39
Washington	11	33,897.86	12,942.87
West Virginia	10	51,080.26	32,454.05
Wisconsin	20	369,194.92	201,790.15
Wyoming	1	1,211.90	
Alberta	18	112,089.17	77,653.64
British Columbia	2	5,709.75	1,921.24
Manitoba	4	21,000.12	
New Brunswick	3	42,285.22	32,500.00
Nova Scotia	2	4,862.04	1,839.16
Ontario	39	141,188.76	59,562.91
Saskatchewan	26	145,222.40	81,815.21
Quebec	28	98,264.53	22,443.28
Foreign	7	21,048.72	5,783.67
	1,001	$6,284,506.49	$2,922,316.28

Twelve

Great Majority Married

Of all the men 798, or 83 per cent., were married. Twenty were divorced or separated and four were widowers. Of the women, seventeen were single, one a divorcee and four were widows.

Eight hundred and twenty-six of the men—nearly 86 per cent.—had dependents. The wives, children, parents and other relatives who were supported entirely or in part by these 826 exceeded 2,000 persons. Eleven of the women had dependents.

Ages

Young and old were among these embezzlers, the youngest being 18 and the oldest 85 years. Nearly 44 per cent. of the men were between the ages of 30 and 40. Thirty-six years and eight months was found to be the average. The average of the women proved to be slightly over 33 years. The youngest was 21 and the oldest 53 years.

Salaries

Were these people poorly paid? Commissions, or salary and commissions, were paid to some. The average, however, in ascertainable cases was $175 a month for the men. The earnings of the women averaged $115 a month.

Notwithstanding that all were trusted and held positions of greater or less responsibility, supervision was exer-

AGE DISTRIBUTION

_____ MEN _____			____ MEN *(Cont.)* ____		
AGE	CASES	PER CENT.	AGE	CASES	PER CENT.
18	1		60	14	
20	2		61	1	
21	4		62	1	
22	13		63	2	
23	10		64	2	
24	20		65	5	
25	18		66	1	
26	26		67	2	
27	48		68	1	
28	31		69	1	
29	61	24.30%	72	1	
30	42		80	1	
31	34		85	1	3.43%
32	55		____ WOMEN ____		
33	33		21	1	
34	38		23	5	
35	38		24	1	
36	64		25	1	
37	48		26	1	
38	51		28	4	34.21%
39	20	43.92%	30	3	
40	52		31	1	
41	29		32	1	
42	29		33	1	
43	20		34	3	
44	9		35	3	
45	20		37	1	
46	11		38	1	36.84%
47	11		40	3	
48	11		42	1	
49	11	21.08%	43	1	
50	17		45	3	
51	4		48	1	
52	12		51	1	
53	12		53	1	28.95%
54	2				
55	7				
56	3				
57	1				
58	9				
59	3	7.27%			

Fourteen

cised by most of the employers. In 91 per cent. of the cases the money or property for which they were responsible was checked at regular intervals.

Period of Embezzlement

What length of time did these embezzlements cover? In many cases a few months. Others extended over a period of years. The average was two and one-half years. In a number of instances large sums of money were taken in a few weeks. The investigation showed a class of cases where a brief period of embezzlement was followed by several years during which no money was taken. In these, the embezzlers, during the interval, attempted to keep their shortages covered up, and tried vainly to replace the money.

Length of Service

Prior to this, perhaps no survey has been made which would disclose whether embezzlers as a rule are newly hired or employes of long standing. The table on the next page reveals that for the most part the 1,001 were old and trusted employes. The length of service of the men was close to six years. As an average, the women had been employed for seven years. Fifty-four per cent. of the men had been employed ten years or more by the concern which suffered the loss. One man had served nearly a half century, and one woman 22 years.

LENGTH OF SERVICE

MEN		WOMEN	
Less than 1 year	83		
1 year	106	1 year	2
2	153	2	1
3	104	3	5
4	74	4	4
5	70	5	5
6	80	6	4
7	41	7	3
8	42	8	2
9	28	9	1
10	30	10	3
11	18	11	1
12	26	12	4
13	13	14	1
14	8	15	1
15	14	22	1
16	5		38
17	7		
18	18		
19	6		
20	7		
21	4		
22	6		
23	1		
24	2		
25	10		
26	1		
30	3		
33	1		
35	1		
45	1		
	963		

Positions Held

Every class of occupation is represented among the 1,001 embezzlers. The men were engaged almost equally in outside and inside positions. The women, with one exception, were employed inside.

Collusion

Did the embezzlers work alone? The records show collusion was present in hardly more than ten per cent. of the cases. Collusion was a factor nearly twice as often, percentage-wise, where women did the embezzling. Often when women were the principals others appeared to benefit from their action; that is to say, the money was spent for the benefit of, or lent to another, or entrusted to some one else for various purposes.

Absconders

The number of those absconding was small—a little more than two per cent. of the total. Twenty-two men and two women disappeared before or at the time their peculations were discovered. And rarely did the employe have the idea of absconding in mind when he first took money. Here it may be well again to point out what has been so often observed—that an embezzler when brought to book, seldom has any of the money left.

OCCUPATIONAL DISTRIBUTION
MEN

POSITIONS	NUMBER
Executive Officers	49
Treasurers	17
Secretaries—Building and Loan Companies, Social Organizations	18
Branch Managers—Groceries, Clothing Stores, Dairies, Auto Accessories, Oil Companies, Loan Companies, Lumber Yards, etc.	201
Clerks in Offices and Stores	52
Accountants and Auditors	17
Bookkeepers	69
Buyers	5
Paymasters	4
Collectors	35
Cashiers	70
Adjusters	4
Investigators	4
Superintendents of Lumber, Coal, Oil Tank Yards	7
Salesmen for Meat, Grocery, Oil, Lumber Companies, and Appliances	115
Representatives of Oil and Gas Companies, Insurance Companies, Motion Picture, Automobile, Specialty and Advertising Companies	262
Merchandise Brokers	2
Time Keeper	1
Drivers and Delivery Men	8
Warehousemen and Stock Clerks	5
Foremen, Laborers	5
Club Stewards	3
National Guard Officers and Ship Captains	5
Attorneys	3
Foreign Consul	1
Optician	1
	963

OCCUPATIONAL DISTRIBUTION
WOMEN

POSITIONS	NUMBER
Cashiers	21
Bookkeepers	9
Collector	1
Store Superintendent	1
Clerk in Office	1
Saleswoman	1
Manager	1
Assistant Treasurer	1
Secretary	1
Auditor	1
	38

Suicides

More committed suicide than absconded. Twenty-eight men and two women took their lives before or at the time their shortages were disclosed. In addition, there were five cases of sudden death, where a verdict of suicide was not given by the coroner. In twenty other cases, shortages were not discovered until the employe had died from apparently natural causes.

In almost as many more, employes who were short in their accounts came to their employers and confessed.

WHY DID THEY STEAL?

MEN

	NUMBER	PER CENT.
Revenge	1	.1
Dishonest Son	1	.1
Blackmail	2	.2
Saving for a Rainy Day	2	.2
Replacing Lost Money	2	.2
Wives	7	.7
Operation of Another Business	13	1.4
Mentally Irresponsible	14	1.5
Inadequate Income	18	1.9
Sickness of Wife, Son or Daughter	57	5.9
Speculation	84	8.7
Women	102	10.6
Bad Business Managers	133	13.8
Accumulation of Debts	156	16.2
Living above their Means	161	16.7
Gambling and/or Drink	169	17.6
Criminal Characters	41	4.2
Total	963	100%

WOMEN

	NUMBER	PER CENT.
Sickness in Family	2	5.3
Dependents	4	10.6
Operation of Another Business	1	2.6
Mentally Irresponsible	3	7.9
Gambling	2	5.3
Men	2	5.3
Accumulation of Debts	11	28.8
Living above their Means	13	34.2
Total	38	100%

Twenty

The Motives

Why did these men and women steal? What do the records show regarding the underlying causes? Were the motives those commonly supposed to be responsible for embezzlements? The accompanying table shows a grouping of various causes which were disclosed by the investigations, following discovery of the defalcations. In many instances, there were several contributing causes—gambling, liquor and women frequently entering into the same cases. Groupings have been made, however, in accordance with the principal one ascribed by the investigator.

A great many detailed confessions form a part of the investigator's report, and much material was gleaned from these. However, the embezzler, in his confession, naturally will put the best possible face on his case, stressing the least reprehensible features of it. So in the main, the investigator's findings, rather than the confessions, have been relied on to determine causes. Hence a fairly accurate picture of the relative importance of the various motives has been embodied in the table.

* * *

Conclusions

The records show that most of these men and women, up to the time their embezzling began, lived normally and honestly. They had clean records in previous employment, as attested by the investigations which preceded their bonding. They had ability. In their previous positions they were subjected to temptation (assuming that every employe at some time is tempted) and resisted it.

They lived among and worked with honest people. They were regarded as honest by those around them, and their employers had no reason to mistrust them. They followed these habits of normal living and honesty well into middle life. They married and supported their families by honest work.

Certainly, on their records, these people are not of the criminal type. The typical criminal is unattached and anti-social, and apt to be feeble-minded or pathological. His habits differ radically from the habits of these embezzlers. As a rule he doesn't associate with honest companions. He does not acquire the habit of living by honest means. He does not marry. And marital status is an important point in differentiating the typically criminal part of our population, for prison records show that those who are married are in the minority. When in prison, too, the difference between the embezzler and the typical criminal has been widely commented on. Embezzlers are model prisoners and are despised by professional criminals. Embezzlers do not usually become recidivists, as do ordinary criminals.

It seems fair to conclude from the facts assembled that men and women employes, up to the point where they "dip into the till," are honest. They do not consider that they are stealing. They do not take with the idea of ultimately absconding. Rather, they feel that they are borrowing, and intend to pay it back. When they take the money, they have a real or fancied need.

A number of typical situations were found to exist. One such is where an emergency creates an urgent need for the money. This plus the opportunity to embezzle proves irresistible. Another is based on debts which through misfortune, carelessness or perhaps petty gambling, have been permitted to accumulate, and the employe "borrows" his employer's money "until his luck changes."

A third situation is created by the more ambitious who think they see an opportunity to make money by speculations, or by starting a business of their own—using their employer's money as capital. Still another is that where the employe contracts the habit of living beyond his means or acquires tastes which his salary does not permit. He then attempts to pay for his expensive tastes and habits on the instalment plan—using his employer as the financing agency.

While some criminal persons appear among the 1,001, their surprisingly small number only emphasizes the fact that the majority are, to begin with, people commonly classed as honest.

At the same time, there is in the character of your typical embezzler, a weakness which prevents him from standing up under temptations and difficulties which others seem successful in overcoming. Go through the table of motives, and for the most part they are merely those things which make up the ordinary hazards of living. However charitably you view them, these people failed while contending with the ordinary hazards of life such as all have to face to a greater or less degree.

The fact that the average age of the embezzlers was in the mid-thirties might support the opinion that these people failed at a period when the difficulties of living were greatest. Again, it might be used as a basis for the theory that the World War had something to do with the delinquency, inasmuch as the principals were placed at an age indicating that many may have had war service.

If any one thing applies to the greatest number of these people, it is that in some manner or other they lived beyond their means, and had they been more careful in this respect would scarcely have become embezzlers.

And trouble really started for many when the first money was taken, for again and again, once peculations began, they increased in frequency and amount and the typical embezzler went from bad to worse—got more and more deeply involved. Indeed, it seems to bear out the old adage to the effect that troubles never come singly. For bad breaks seem to have followed one upon another for some of these people, after they had made the first false step. If money taken was used for betting on a sure winner, the horse ran last. If taken to pay the butcher, the grocer demanded his bill be paid before that which went to pay the butcher could be put back into the till. Stocks purchased with the hope of getting rich quickly took a slump and the embezzler was wiped out—and the employer's funds could not be replaced as originally intended. If the money was taken because of domestic trouble, that trouble seemed promptly to become more complex or aggravated. Or if the employe began to live beyond his means in one respect, a growing appetite in another direction demanded to be appeased.

No doubt those who become embezzlers have a greater tendency toward dishonesty than those who remain honest. Still, under more favorable circumstances and better safeguards many of those who became embezzlers would have continued honest.

Incidentally, the division between the sexes represented —963 men and 38 women—can not be used as a basis for conclusions on the relative honesty of men and women. There are fewer women employed, and probably a smaller percentage, relatively, attain to positions of responsibility. Moreover, women who attain to such positions are as a rule more closely supervised.

Among the Borrowers

A Cashier Lives Beyond His Means

No. 12-MF-11 was 45 years old. He had been cashier of a motor company in Wisconsin for 16 years. His record was exceptionally good. He was married, and had a daughter attending college. However, for several years, he embezzled from his employers, because he was living beyond his means.

> Result—He lost his position; his wife divorced him; his daughter is a waitress in a restaurant.

Amount of embezzlement—$8,477.16.

Ambitious Executive

No. 180039 was one of the best known business men in a certain Ohio city. For ten years he was executive vice-president of a finance company. Eager to become rich quickly, he secretly established a business of his own, using funds belonging to his employer as capital. The new business did not prosper.

Amount of embezzlement—$46,948.00.

Death Reveals an Embezzler

No. 161434 was for 25 years employed by a casket company in Kentucky. At the time of his sudden death, he was the treasurer. A checkup of his books which had not been previously audited showed that he had been embezzling for a considerable period.

Amount of embezzlement—$16,000.00.

Keeping Up Appearances

No. 179996 was employed for 12 years by a large manufacturing concern in New York State. He was on intimate terms with and was trusted implicitly by the company's officers. He was 40 years old, and had a wife and eight-year-old child. He was a churchgoer, member of several lodges, and in his private life was considered a model of propriety. However, he wanted to make an impression, and lived beyond his means — embezzled to keep up appearances. When his defalcations were discovered, he resented any implication that he was a thief and stated that given time he would have replaced the money.

Amount of embezzlement—$10,304.75.

Promising Engineer

No. 170101, employed for six years by a contracting firm, was sent to South America because of exceptional ability. He did the work, but the South American government complained of a shortage in the fund set up for the project. The engineer had made away with the money. He stated that he was lonely in a strange land, and needed funds for amusement. Following exposure of his theft, he disappeared into the interior of the country.

Amount of embezzlement—$16,061.73.

Wife's Suspicion

No. 182770 was a single woman, 31 years old, employed by a concern in Oregon for 10 years as bookkeeper and cashier at $125 a month. She dressed well, owned a car, maintained an expensive apartment. Finally, she lent a fellow employe $1,000, which aroused the suspicion of the wife of the borrower. The wife talked, and the defalcation was disclosed.

Amount of embezzlement—$23,735.57.

The Market Went Down

No. 200579 was assistant treasurer of an Illinois construction company. He was 42 years old, had a wife and child. His salary was $900 a month. He was implicitly trusted. He had helped to found the company, and had installed the bookkeeping system. However, he took the company's funds when his private speculations in the stock market turned out unsatisfactorily.

Amount of embezzlement—$15,858.56.

Shipping Clerk Perfects a System

No. 4-MF-2 was only a shipping clerk in a New York produce company. He was 41 years old, and had 3 children. To support his family in a manner which his salary would not permit, he devised during his 8 years' employment a system for appropriating goods and reselling them for his own benefit. His system baffled his employers—more than that, it baffled detectives the employers engaged. Goods continued to come in one door and go out the other, and they could not discover who was responsible. Finally, other employes divulged the system and the total of the loss astonished the owners.

Amount of embezzlement—$34,500.00.

From Office Boy to Embezzler

No. 188336 began as office boy, and rose to assistant office manager for a New York association of credit men after 16 years of service. Among other things, he purchased the stamps, with a check drawn to his order. However, he spent less for the stamps than the amount of money he drew. Not until a stamp machine was installed was his dishonesty discovered. He admitted that his peculations averaged fifty to sixty dollars a week, and stated that he used the money for living expenses and for pleasure.

Amount of embezzlement—$9,722.86.

Two Families to Support

No. 34-MF-4 was for more than ten years general agent for an insurance company in a Kentucky city. He had a wife and recently married daughter whose household he supported in addition to his own. For this his earnings were not sufficient, so he began embezzling with the result that he was sentenced to 14 years in the penitentiary.

Amount of embezzlement—$15,000.00.

Fifty-one and Unmarried

No. 190571 was a single woman, 51 years old, and for many years cashier and bookkeeper of a hospital in Minnesota at $100 a month. She lived beyond her means, and embezzled the institution's funds to pay her bills. A friend was given $1,000 of the money for speculation. It was lost. When the defalcation was discovered, this employe registered at a hotel under an assumed name and committed suicide.

Amount of embezzlement—$6,500.00.

He Ran the Business

No. 191439 was assistant treasurer for an Indiana tool making concern which had been inherited by four members of a family who were more interested in other pursuits than in operating their business. The assistant treasurer, therefore, came to run it for them, and in addition attended to most of their private estates as well. This went on for seven years. After a time, however, the assistant treasurer began to work more particularly for his own interests.

Amount of embezzlement—$25,856.82.

Clerk Meets "Other Woman"

No. 170978 was a clerk for a battery company in Wisconsin. He was 27 years of age, married and had one child. However, married life irked him, and he sought diversion. He met the "other woman" and soon found his salary was not enough to satisfy her and keep his wife and child. Then his embezzling began.

Amount of embezzlement—$27,000.00.

Domestic Trouble

No. 206025 was 63 years old, and had been secretary of a realty concern in Colorado for 13 years. His life was not a happy one. His wife "nagged" him, and his son was continually in trouble. In one way and another, they cost this man a lot of money. He spent his own and that of the realty company as well. What he took from the till, he replaced when he could, but the shortage mounted over a period of several years. Finally, it could be covered up no longer.

Amount of embezzlement—$16,547.76.

Good Showing

No. 36-MF-14 was branch manager of a food company in Missouri for 6 years. He was 35 years old, had a wife and 3 children. An audit showed a large shortage. This man then confessed, stating that "in order to make a good showing, I started making entries in the accounts receivable ledger, showing payments for a number of delinquent or bad accounts where no payments had actually been made. I never profited by receiving any remuneration on any of these accounts." However, he caused a large loss to his employers, because of his poor business methods and false records.

Amount of embezzlement—$29,000.00.

Community Leader

No. 161247 was prominent in a Massachusetts community. He was 56 years old and married. Besides being treasurer of a cemetery, he was president of a bank, and member of the board of a home for the aged. He had served for 30 years as treasurer of the cemetery, the funds of which he embezzled. At the time his defalcation was discovered, it was disclosed that the entire amount had been lost in stock market speculation.

Amount of embezzlement—$10,768.67.

Lost the Money He Stole

No. 187060 was a Canadian, 36 years old. He had a wife and 3 children. He worked for a wholesale company. After nearly 9 years of service, he heard his company was about to sell out its business. He feared the loss of his position, and took the money to tide him over the period of idleness which he feared would ensue. For a time, he carried this money about with him, but had the misfortune to lose the entire amount. Meanwhile an audit disclosed the embezzlement.

Amount of embezzlement—$2,183.29.

New Jersey Stock Clerk

No. 161098 was 40 years old and had been employed for 17 years as a stock clerk for an electric supply company. He handled no cash but some of the machine parts in his stock room contained platinum. An acquaintance who was in the garage business suggested that such parts could be turned into cash. The clerk began to steal them, and the tempter sold them.

Amount of embezzlement—$23,511.57.

Trouble and More Trouble

No. 7-MF-3 was married and at the age of 40 had 3 dependents. He had been employed as a bookkeeper for 8 years by a wholesale concern in Massachusetts, at $120 a month. Troubles, however, beset this man. His wife had a cancer. His children were continually ill. Hospital and doctor bills were higher than he could pay. No real audit was ever made of his accounts, so he "borrowed" from his employers to pay his bills.

Amount of embezzlement—$2,011.98.

Down South

No. 168774 was 24 years old. He had married a Sunday school teacher and had been employed four years by a real estate concern in Alabama. Living beyond his means caused him to take his company's money which was not discovered for some time, as his employers said "we had not made a complete audit for some time, due to the confidence we had in this man. His reputation had always been splendid."

Amount of embezzlement—$2,643.00.

Went off with the "Other Woman"

No. 178660 was married and 52 years of age. He lived in Illinois. For five years he was office manager for a coal company. He had a good reputation and had been married for 27 years, but for 5 months prior to the discovery of his shortage, he had been staying away from home every night. Finally, his wife learned that he was spending the time at the home of a married woman, whose husband was away. The wife threatened divorce action. So when the defalcation was discovered, this man went off with the other woman.

Amount of embezzlement—$3,039.62.

Widow Needed $3.80

No. 198113 was a widow 42 years old. For 15 years, she was employed in a department store. She confessed that she first took $3.80 of her employer's money. She needed this amount badly, and when she took it, intended to pay it back from her next pay check—but she never did. Instead, she took other amounts subsequently. Finally, the situation got beyond her, and her peculations were discovered.

Amount of embezzlement—$1,363.94.

Bookkeeper in Love

No. 186457 was bookkeeper for a manufacturing concern for 5 years. He was married, but at the age of 44 fell in love with a young girl. He used his employer's money to buy her an automobile and other expensive presents, and drank himself into a state that bordered on insanity.

Amount of embezzlement—$10,000.00.

Bought His Wife Diamonds

No. 163073 was 50 years old. He supported a wife and two children by working as an agent for an oil company in Georgia. When a shortage in his accounts was discovered, he killed himself. Subsequent investigation showed that he had mortgaged his house for more than it was worth, that he owed almost everyone in town, and that he had bought his wife over $3,000 worth of diamonds. The wife said the shortage was caused by giving credit to customers who didn't pay. The investigator found this untrue.

Amount of embezzlement—$1,093.76.

Burned the Office

No. 185497 was sent as a branch manager to a European country by a moving picture company. He was 42 years old, had a wife and child. He fell in love with a girl who worked in his office. When she was discharged, he continued to pay her salary from his own pocket, and began to drink and gamble recklessly. His employers began to investigate his business affairs, whereupon he burned up the office with himself in it.

Amount of embezzlement—$3,507.55.

A County Judge

No. 184902 was one of the organizers of a Missouri building and loan association and acted as its secretary and treasurer for more than 10 years. He was 64 years old. He had a wife and 3 children. He was presiding judge in the County Court and head of an insurance business. He used the association's money to live extravagantly. His embezzlement was not discovered until after his death.

Amount of embezzlement—$10,349.90.

Wanted to Marry Again

No. 181960 was divorced from his wife but he had to pay her alimony from salary earned as branch manager for a mid-west stores company. He was 36 years old and wanted to marry again, but had to make some settlement with his wife before doing so. He took his employer's money to make the settlement.

Amount of embezzlement—$4,467.05.

President Ends a Suicide

No. 181333 was president of his company in Wisconsin. He was 60 years old, married and had two children. He lost money in the stock market and then took from his company money enough to settle these losses, pay his life insurance premiums and his chauffeur. Then he committed suicide.

Amount of embezzlement—$271,777.81.

The Other Woman Got the Money

No. 184091 was 35 years old and married. He worked for 3 years as bookkeeper for a lumber company in Louisiana. During this time, he had an affair with "another woman." Her demands took every cent he could get his hands on. This drove him to embezzle and later to commit suicide. The shortage was disclosed after his death.

Amount of embezzlement—$1,799.73.

Wine, Women and Song

No. 199267 was secretary of a Florida real estate company. He was 43 years old and had been employed by this company for 17 years. His business reputation was the best. He was married and had 2 children. But he began running around with other women, drinking and frequenting night clubs. One night while in a beach party where there was considerable drinking his companion, a married woman, was drowned. He paid some of the money he took from his employers to this woman's husband as a settlement.

Amount of embezzlement—$29,382.54.

Religious Cultist

No. 55-MF-2 was a widow, 45 years of age. She was employed for 12 years at $175 a month by a finance company in Nevada. In addition, she was a stockholder in the company. No audit was ever made of her books. She lived a quiet life, spent little money on herself. She had the best of associates. But she was over-religious and steadily embezzled for the benefit of a man who headed a religious cult of which she was a member. She called him her "apostle of truth." The apostle spent the money in California, mostly on another woman.

Amount of embezzlement—$13,742.75.

He Always Lost

No. 11-MF-108 was 31 years old, was married and had 2 children. He was employed as a cashier for a motor company. He discovered a shortage of $400 in his accounts. He feared he would lose his job if this were disclosed, so he covered it up for several months, trying to replace the shortage in the meantime by gambling at the race track with money he took from his company. This was a failure, for he always lost. Finally, in desperation, he voluntarily confessed the shortage and his additional peculations to his employer.

Amount of embezzlement—$1,157.00.

Woman Cashier's Troubles

No. 172818 was a single woman, 21 years old. She was employed as a cashier in a mid-western retail store. She needed money to pay for an operation of an embarrassing nature. To avoid telling her family of her condition, she arranged it by taking her employer's money.

Amount of embezzlement—$1,698.00.

Airplane Line on the Side

No. 162170 was 58 years old. He had a wife and child. He was vice-president of a supply company in Louisiana, and acted as its cashier. He ran an airplane line on the side, bought an expensive house to live in and bought another in his wife's name. To finance these matters, he embezzled from his company. This was not so difficult as the president was his best friend and trusted him implicitly. When shortage was disclosed, No. 162170 killed himself.

Amount of embezzlement—$23,000.00.

To Make an Impression

No. 181315 was 26 years old. He was employed by a Pennsylvania wholesale concern at a salary of $30.00 a week. He told the girl he was courting that he was making $65.00 a week. And proceeded to give evidence to support his story by spending all his money as well as some of his employer's on her. He also did some little gambling, which proved costly to his company.

Amount of embezzlement—$7,134.32.

Night Life

No. 167014 was credit manager and assistant treasurer of a large manufacturing company. That was his occupation during the day. At night he spent his time in the city's gay spots. The money that he spent in these places was his employer's money. When a shortage was discovered, company officials were exceedingly loath to believe that their assistant treasurer had taken the money. His business reputation had been excellent. He was married, had 2 children and was 36 years old.

Amount of embezzlement—$26,668.21.

Financing a Fiancee

No. 206537 was 22 years old, and was employed for over 3 years as cashier for a transportation company in Missouri. He confessed, "I stole small amounts at first, thinking to replace them later out of my salary. This I found impossible to do as my shortage kept growing and reached a point where I couldn't possibly take care of it." No. 206537 was married two months before his embezzling was discovered and the investigations showed that the money stolen from his employers had gone for expenses in courting the girl he married.

Amount of embezzlement—$2,472.86.

Declined Promotion

No. 196919 was employed for 22 years by a manufacturing concern and served as its branch manager. He was married, and 66 years old. No. 196919 was thought of so highly, and his work so eminently satisfactory, that officers of his company urged him to come into the home office to fill an executive position, which he declined. The reason was disclosed at the time of his death when a stock shortage was discovered, and investigation showed that the company's goods had been disposed of to provide money for gambling.

Amount of embezzlement—$4,699.38.

Friends Wanted Their Money

No. 205057 was employed for a year by an automobile company, at a salary of $100 a month. He was 57 years old and married. His wife was an invalid and prior to taking this position, he had been out of work for some time and had practically lived on money borrowed from his friends. When he obtained this position, the friends clamored for their money, which he could not pay back as fast as they demanded it.

Amount of embezzlement—$1,140.10.

Perfect Bookkeeping

No. 205478 was for 16 years cashier of a public service company in Alaska, at a salary of $232.50 a month. He was 59 years old, married, had one child. Living beyond his means caused him to embezzle, although the employers stated, "We had a system of bookkeeping which we considered required no audit, as we always thought it would be impossible for any employe to misappropriate funds without almost immediate detection."

Amount of embezzlement—$5,312.09.

CPSIA information can be obtained
at www.ICGtesting.com
Printed in the USA
BVHW031753110922
646766BV00019B/221